BUILT FOR SPEED

BUILT FOR SPEED

The Extraordinary, Enigmatic Cheetah

by Sharon Elaine Thompson

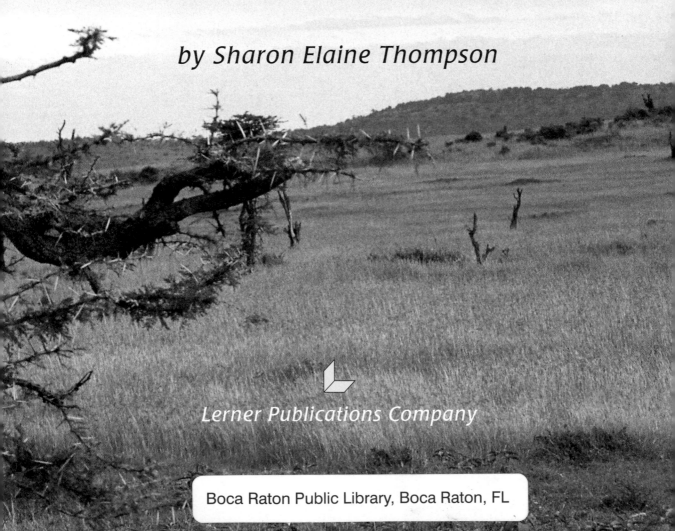

Lerner Publications Company

For Warren Deane Thomas, D.V.M.,
former director of the Los Angeles Zoo,
who fueled my curiosity about animals,
and
for the docents at the Los Angeles Zoo,
in gratitude for five years of camaraderie.

Acknowledgments

I would like to thank Dr. Tim Caro, Dr. Stephen J. O'Brien, Dr. Warren D. Thomas, Dr. Mitch Bush, Jack Grisham, Willie Labuschagne, and Ann Van Dyk for their patience in answering my questions about cheetahs. Thanks to Joelle Goldman, whose wonderful editing strengthened the manuscript, and to Margaret Goldstein for her support and encouragement. In addition, I am grateful to Dr. Caro and Dr. Thomas for reading parts of the manuscript for accuracy. Any omissions or errors, however, are the responsibility of the author.

Lerner Publications Company
A Division of Lerner Publishing Group
241 First Avenue North
Minneapolis, MN 55401 U.S.A.

Website address: www.lernerbooks.com

Library of Congress Cataloging-in-Publication Data

Thompson, Sharon Elaine, 1952–
    Built for speed : the extraordinary, enigmatic cheetah / by Sharon
Elaine Thompson.
        p.   cm.
    Includes bibliographical references (p.) and index.
    Summary: Describes the habitat, physical characteristics, and
behavior of the cheetah, as well as efforts to ensure the continued
existence of this fastest land mammal.
    ISBN 0-8225-2854-1 (alk. paper)
    1. Cheetah-Juvenile literature. [1. Cheetah. 2. Endangered
species.] I. Title.
QL737.C23T4737   1998
599.75'9-dc21   96-51094

Manufactured in the United States of America
2 3 4 5 6 7 – JR – 05 04 03 02 01 00

Contents

A cheetah chases a Thomson's gazelle across the African savanna.

Introduction

The treeless East African savanna shimmers in the summer heat. A herd of Thomson's gazelles, a type of antelope, nibbles quietly on the dry grass. There are few trees or rocks to hide the Tommies from predators. Instead, the antelopes are protected by the large number of animals in the herd. If danger threatens, one of the gazelles is sure to spot it in time for the whole herd to run away. Healthy adult antelopes can outrun most predators.

But crouched in the long grass near the herd is one hunter the Tommies cannot outrun—a cheetah. Its spotted yellow coat helps it blend into the grass as it creeps closer to the grazing animals. Suddenly the cheetah stands up, startling the gazelles. The frightened herd begins to run. With stunning speed, the cheetah runs down the antelope it has chosen as its prey. The cheetah bites the young gazelle's throat to strangle it. The rest of the herd stops in the distance and begins to graze again under the hot sun.

The cheetah is the world's fastest land mammal. But speed does not guarantee survival. In fact, the cheetah's biology and way of life make it difficult for the cheetah to survive. Many male cheetahs are infertile—unable to father cubs. Only 5 percent of cheetah cubs live to become adults. The remainder die from disease, starvation, or attacks by other predators, such as lions. The swift cats have been victims of humans, too. They have been hunted for their fur and destroyed as threats to livestock. Their hunting grounds have been fenced in by farmers and cattle ranchers. Where cheetahs cannot run free, they cannot survive. In much of their range, cheetahs have lost the race against extinction and have disappeared. Cheetahs are considered an endangered species.

Although humans have contributed to the cheetah's disappearance, human beings are making an effort to see that cheetahs do not die out altogether. In some areas, cheetahs are protected by law. Zoos and animal parks in Europe, Africa, and the United States are breeding and raising the cats. Scientists are studying them to learn more about their behavior. The more we know about cheetahs, the better we can help the cheetahs that still run free.

Living on the Edge of Extinction

The cheetah is considered an endangered animal. "Endangered" animals are in immediate risk of becoming extinct. They could die out within a very short time—five to ten years—if humans do not take steps to protect them.

Animals can become endangered as the result of hunting or disease. They can become endangered when their habitat is reduced or destroyed. Often, animals become endangered because of human activities. But animals can become extinct due to natural changes in the environment, too. For example, warming temperatures at the end of the last ice age (about 10,000 years ago) may have caused the extinction of animals such as the woolly mammoth.

Sometimes animals are described as "threatened." This means that they are not in immediate danger of extinction, but the animals or their habitats are under pressure—usually from humans. Threatened animals may become endangered if humans do not control trade in those animals or protect their habitats.

It is necessary to have international agreement about the protection of animals. Migrating animals, such as caribou, songbirds, and wildebeest, may move from country to country. Other animals, such as seals and whales, live in oceans used by all countries.

In 1973, representatives of 80 countries signed the Convention on International Trade in Endangered Species of Wild Fauna and Flora (CITES). By the mid-1990s, more than 120 countries had signed the treaty. These countries agreed to follow the CITES guidelines, which are put out in a publication called the *Red Data Book*.

The *Red Data Book* includes three appendices, each of which lists a particular category of animals. Endangered animals are listed in Appendix I. All trade in these animals, or products made from parts of these animals (such as skins and horns), is prohibited. Appendix II lists animals that may be hunted or exported if the hunter or exporter has a government permit. Appendix III restricts international trade in individuals of some species coming from certain countries. The animals listed here are rare in these particular countries, although they may not be rare somewhere else.

The CITES treaty cannot guarantee protection of endangered animals. The governments of the countries have to do that themselves. Not all countries have signed the CITES agreement. And even those countries who have signed it do not always abide by its rules.

Sometimes a government thinks that protecting particular animals will hurt its economy. Perhaps its people earn money taking hunters out to find animals such as cheetahs. The government may be afraid that the protected animals will attack livestock or destroy crops. It may cost too much to set up and protect animal preserves. And sometimes the government does not consider the animals to be endangered in its country. It sees no reason to protect them.

Cheetahs live throughout the open plains of central and southern Africa.

Chapter 1

A Most Unusual Cat

Suppose someone told you about a large cat that was unable to roar, had claws that were blunt like a dog's, could not climb trees well, was very timid, chirped like a bird, and could run as fast as a speeding car. What would you say? You would say it was a cheetah.

The first cheetahs probably evolved in Asia, but fossils show that many different kinds of cheetahs once lived all over the world. Between two and four million years ago, for example, a species of cat called *Acinonyx pardinensis* lived in Europe. These giant cheetahs may have weighed as much as 200 pounds, which is twice as much as modern cheetahs weigh. In the mid-Pleistocene epoch (about a million years ago), a smaller cheetah species called *Acinonyx intermedius* roamed from China through India and the Middle East into southern Europe. *Acinonyx trumani* and *Acinonyx studeri,* species that were about the size of the modern cheetah, lived in North America. About 20,000 years ago, during the last ice age, all species of cheetahs died out except for *Acinonyx jubatus,* the common cheetah.

In modern times, cheetahs are found primarily in central and southern Africa, in the countries of Namibia, Botswana, Zambia, Zimbabwe, Tanzania, Kenya, and South Africa. Researchers have reported that there are some cheetahs left in Iran. Cheetahs live on open plains, such as grasslands or deserts, where they have plenty of room to stretch their legs. They need to be fast because they usually hunt antelopes, fast-running animals that live throughout Asia and Africa.

The cheetah is unique among cats, whether they are large or small, domestic or wild. Most cats are solitary. They live alone except when it is time to mate. Lions, which live in groups called prides, are truly social cats. Only cheetahs are both solitary and social. Some cheetahs live alone, while others live in small groups. Most large cats are nocturnal, which means they are active at night. Only cheetahs are primarily diurnal, or active during the day. Most large cats stalk their prey and pounce on it after a short run. Only cheetahs run their prey down over an extended distance. All cats except the cheetah have fully retractile claws. When relaxed, the claws slide back into claw sheaths. This helps to keep the claws sharp. The cheetah's claws aren't fully retractile, so they become worn down through contact with the ground. They are blunt, like a dog's claws.

Cheetahs have a lighter physical structure than other large cats. Their jaws are weaker, in proportion to their size, than the jaws of other cats. Most cats kill prey with a powerful bite to the back of the animal's neck or skull. Cheetahs kill very small prey that way, but most often they use their jaws to grab the animal's throat and strangle it.

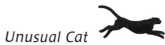

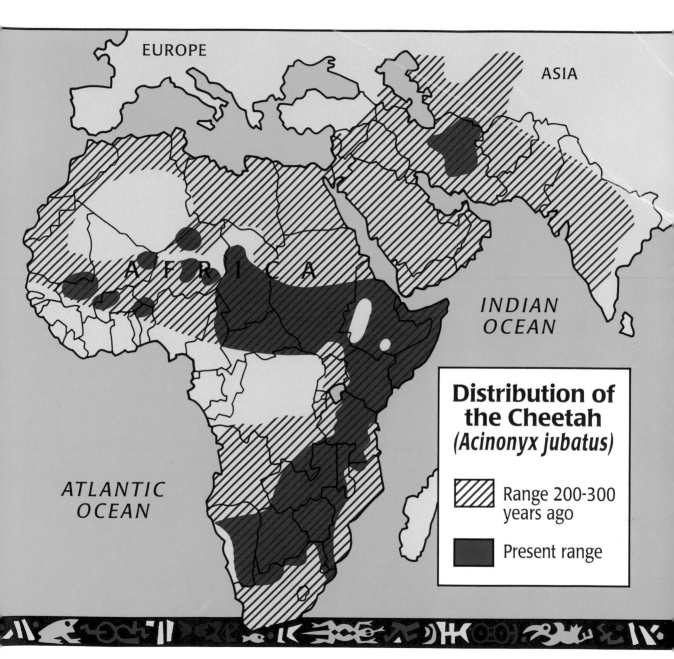

Distribution of the Cheetah
(*Acinonyx jubatus*)

Range 200-300 years ago

Present range

Antelopes—Cheetahs' Favorite Fast Food

Herds of antelopes are a familiar sight on the plains of Africa. The herbivores move across the land, browsing on the leaves of shrubs and trees, or grazing on grasses and low-growing plants. They range in size from the tiny dik-dik of southern Africa, which weighs 10.5 pounds and is only 15 inches high at the shoulder, to the giant eland of Africa, which weighs 1,650 pounds and is almost 6 feet high at the shoulder.

Antelopes are prey for lions, leopards, cheetahs, wild dogs, and hyenas, so they are always alert. Because they could be threatened by a predator at any moment, baby antelopes are up on their feet and ready to run shortly after birth.

Most antelopes look a little like deer, but they are actually in the same family as cows, goats, water buffalo, and sheep. These animals must always be ready to run from danger, so they take little time to chew their food when they eat. They are ruminants—they swallow their food with very little chewing and store it in one chamber of their stomach. Later, when they are resting, they cough the food up into their mouth and chew it again.

All male antelopes have horns, and so do the females of most species. Horns are made up of a bony core covered by a sheath of keratin, the material that fingernails and hair are made of. Horns grow throughout an antelope's life. They are not branched, nor do they fall off each year like the antlers of a deer. Some antelopes, such as the duiker, have tiny, spikelike horns. Others have very large and ornate horns. The greater kudu, for example, has twisted horns that corkscrew up to a length of 4.5 feet! Horns can be used as weapons when predators attack. Male antelopes may use their horns to fight other males over territory or females.

Antelopes live throughout Africa and Asia. They usually live in open grasslands, but small antelopes, such as duikers, live in heavy forest. The pronghorn of North America is sometimes called an antelope—it is mentioned in the song "Home on the Range." But the pronghorn is not related to the antelopes of Africa. It is in a family by itself.

A herd of gazelles and wildebeest migrating across Tanzania's Serengeti Plain

Breaking Up the Family

Cats are all members of one family of animals called Felidae. Felidae is divided into five groups, each of which is called a genus. Most cats, including the domestic cat, are in the genus *Felis*. Cats in this genus are commonly called "small cats." Lions, tigers, leopards, jaguars, and snow leopards, or "big cats," are in the genus *Panthera*. These are the cats that roar.

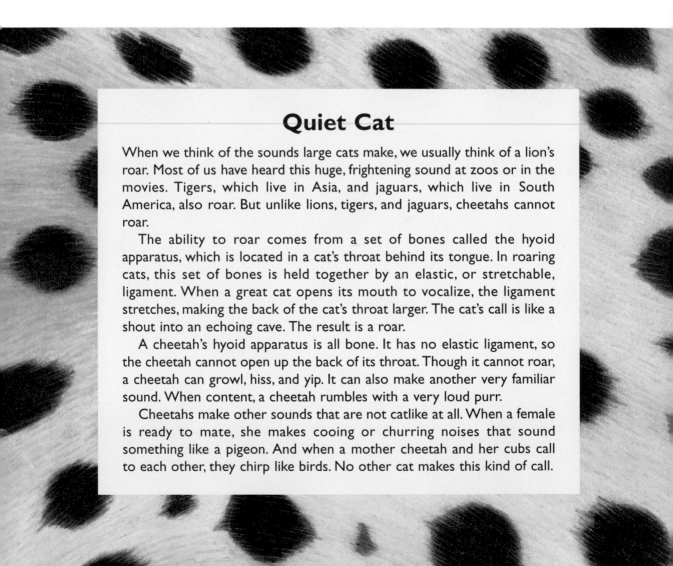

Quiet Cat

When we think of the sounds large cats make, we usually think of a lion's roar. Most of us have heard this huge, frightening sound at zoos or in the movies. Tigers, which live in Asia, and jaguars, which live in South America, also roar. But unlike lions, tigers, and jaguars, cheetahs cannot roar.

The ability to roar comes from a set of bones called the hyoid apparatus, which is located in a cat's throat behind its tongue. In roaring cats, this set of bones is held together by an elastic, or stretchable, ligament. When a great cat opens its mouth to vocalize, the ligament stretches, making the back of the cat's throat larger. The cat's call is like a shout into an echoing cave. The result is a roar.

A cheetah's hyoid apparatus is all bone. It has no elastic ligament, so the cheetah cannot open up the back of its throat. Though it cannot roar, a cheetah can growl, hiss, and yip. It can also make another very familiar sound. When content, a cheetah rumbles with a very loud purr.

Cheetahs make other sounds that are not catlike at all. When a female is ready to mate, she makes cooing or churring noises that sound something like a pigeon. And when a mother cheetah and her cubs call to each other, they chirp like birds. No other cat makes this kind of call.

Cheetahs are by themselves in a separate genus, *Acinonyx*. The cheetah's full scientific name is *Acinonyx jubatus*. *Acinonyx* comes from Greek words that can mean either "unmoving claw" or "thorn claw." *Jubatus* is a Latin word that means mane or crest. (Young cheetahs have a short mane that runs down their backs.)

The word "cheetah" comes from the Hindi word *chita*, which means "spotted one." The cheetah has coarse, light-yellow fur that pales to white on its chest and stomach. Its coat is covered with small rounded spots of very dark brown or black. A dark "tear streak" runs from the inside corners of its amber-colored eyes to the corners of its mouth. Some researchers think that the dark fur under a cheetah's eyes cuts down on the glare of the sun reflecting from the cheetah's light-colored face.

The Hunting Leopard

Cheetahs' graceful bodies and stunning speed have always fascinated human beings. Cheetahs are the fastest-running animals on earth. They are able to run at speeds up to 70 miles per hour. Because cheetahs are easy to tame, for thousands of years people kept cheetahs as pets and used them to hunt antelopes and deer. The practice began as many as 5,000 years ago in ancient Mesopotamia (parts of Iraq, Syria, and Turkey). The ancient Abyssinians (residents of modern-day Ethiopia), Persians (residents of modern-day Iran), and Arabians hunted with cheetahs, too. In the late thirteenth century, the Italian explorer and adventurer Marco Polo reported that Mongol Emperor Kublai Khan kept these "long-legged leopards" at his court in China.

Royalty in ancient Egypt also captured and tamed cheetahs and used them to hunt antelopes. The cats became favorite hunting animals, as popular as dogs. But the Egyptians also considered the cheetah sacred. They believed that fleet-footed cheetahs carried the spirits of the dead to the underworld. When archaeologists opened King Tutankhamen's tomb in 1922, they found many paintings and sculptures of cheetahs.

The sport of hunting with cheetahs may have reached its height in India during the 1500s. Cheetahs were so popular there that Emperor Akbar the Great kept more than 1,000 cheetahs on the palace grounds. Large crowds would often gather to watch the cheetahs chase their prey. When a cat was successful in the hunt, the crowd would clap and cheer. One cheetah reportedly jumped over a 70-foot-wide ravine while chasing a deer. The people named it "Chief of the Cheetahs."

Cheetahs were taken to the hunt wearing hoods, so they would not see their prey and start the chase too soon. The hunters took the cheetah to within 900 feet of a herd of antelopes. Then they removed the hood and the cheetah was off!

Some hunters trained cheetahs to hunt only male antelopes. If a cheetah killed a male, it was allowed to eat some of the animal's meat. If it killed a female, it got none of the kill. Within six months, the cheetahs learned to select only male antelopes so that they would get their reward. Other hunters had a different reward for the cheetah. While the cheetah was still holding the antelope's throat with its teeth, the hunter cut open a vein in the antelope's back leg. The hunter caught the blood in a bowl and gave that to the cheetah to drink. Then the hunter carefully took away the cat's catch.

During the Middle Ages, European royalty took up the Eastern sport of hunting with cheetahs. Europeans called the prized

A detail from the fresco The Journey of the Magi, *by Benozzo Gozzoli (1420-1498), showing medieval riders with captive cheetahs*

cats "hunting leopards" because they were spotted like leopards and were used to catch game. The Europeans used cheetahs to hunt deer. The hooded cheetahs rode to the hunt in style—sitting on a special pillow on the back of the hunter's horse!

Even in the early twentieth century, humans tried to use cheetahs for entertainment. The fast cats were raced against greyhounds, which can reach speeds of 35 to 40 miles per hour. The greyhounds chased a mechanical rabbit around a track, but the cheetahs wouldn't. The cheetahs kept cutting across the infield of the track to catch the rabbit on the other side!

Their speed, grace, and beauty have made cheetahs popular with human hunters for thousands of years. But helping humans hunt for sport is different from hunting to survive. In the wild, hunting is a very serious business. That is why cheetahs are built for speed.

A Helpful Hunter

An African legend tells how the cheetahs got their tear streaks. It seems that a mother cheetah went off to hunt one day, leaving her four cubs hidden. But an evil man was watching her and saw where she had hidden the little ones. He stole the cubs while their mother was away. When the mother discovered her cubs were missing, she began to cry. She cried so hard that, to this day, all cheetahs have tear tracks on their faces.

The story goes on to explain that a kind man came along and asked the mother cheetah why she was crying. She told him about her stolen cubs. The man was angry that someone would take the cheetah's youngsters, and he went to search for them. He found them and returned them to their mother. She was so grateful that she promised that future generations of cheetahs would be loyal to humans. This legend may have begun as a way to explain why cheetahs are easily tamed.

A cheetah's dark tear streaks may reduce glare, helping the cat to see in bright sunlight.

A cheetah's body is ideally suited for high-speed chases.

Chapter 2

Born to Run

The one thing most people know about cheetahs is that they are fast. At peak speed, some cheetahs can hit 70 miles per hour. That's more than a mile a minute—faster than most cars go on the highway. High-speed running takes a huge amount of energy. As a result, cheetahs can run at top speed for only about 200 to 600 yards (about a third of a mile). On average, cheetahs cruise at speeds of 35 to 55 miles per hour, depending on the speed of the animal they are chasing.

Cheetahs are fast from the moment they start to run. Some researchers claim that a cheetah can accelerate from a standing position to 35 or 45 miles per hour in just two seconds! One scientist wrote that the cheetah's initial speed "is astounding— it shoots forward like an arrow from a bow."

A cheetah needs to be fast because the antelopes it hunts are swift runners, able to hit 35 to 40 miles per hour. The cheetah must be even faster in order to catch them. Because a cheetah has to run to eat, it is a running machine. Almost every part of a cheetah's body—from its nose to its feet to its tail—is designed for speed.

Breathing Hard

Running animals need lots of energy. They get it from nutrients contained in the food they eat. They store the energy in their bodies. During a cheetah's burst of speed, its muscles release stored energy in a series of chemical reactions. Oxygen, one of many gases found in the air, is vital to these reactions.

Animals breathe hard when they run. They pull in up to 40 times more air while running than when they are at rest. The increased supply of oxygen fuels the chemical reactions that convert nutrients to energy and helps running animals keep up their speed. The bodies of animals whose lives depend on running produce energy more efficiently than those of other animals. The systems that carry nutrients and oxygen to cheetahs' muscles are somewhat larger and stronger than those of animals that do not run frequently or at such high speeds.

A cheetah's speed begins in its nose. Large nostrils and nasal cavities, hollow areas in the upper part of the nose, allow the cheetah to take in a great deal of air—and oxygen—quickly. The air passes through the cheetah's bronchial tubes and lungs, both of which are larger than those of other cats the cheetah's size.

In the lungs, the air flows into smaller and smaller passages until it reaches millions of tiny air sacs called alveoli. The alveoli are surrounded with very small blood vessels called capillaries. Oxygen passes through the thin wall separating the alveoli from the capillaries and enters the blood. The oxygen-rich blood moves to the cheetah's powerful heart, which pumps the blood through the cat's body. Strong, muscular blood vessels carry the blood quickly to the cheetah's hard-working muscles.

Animals store energy in their bodies in the form of sugars called carbohydrates. Carbohydrates are made up of carbon, hydrogen, and oxygen. When the cheetah begins to run, chemicals called enzymes break the carbohydrates into carbon dioxide (made up of carbon and oxygen) and hydrogen. This chemical reaction releases energy. Part of the energy escapes as heat, and

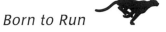

the rest is used by the cheetah's muscles to power its run.

Oxygen from the blood combines with the released hydrogen to make water. At the same time, the blood collects the released carbon dioxide and carries it back to the lungs. The carbon dioxide goes through the alveoli, the bronchial tubes, and the nose as the cheetah exhales. This oxygen-carbon dioxide cycle has to happen very quickly and efficiently. Without enough oxygen, or with too much carbon dioxide in its blood, the cheetah cannot hit top speed and will tire very quickly.

After a cheetah finishes its chase, you can tell it has been working hard. Its rate of respiration is very high—between 130 and 150 breaths per minute! (When resting, humans breathe at a rate of only 10 to 15 breaths per minute.) A cheetah often breathes so fast that observers have trouble counting the number of breaths it takes.

Bone-Deep Speed

Breathing, of course, is not the only key to speed. The cheetah's bones also make it swift. The cheetah's bones are slender and lightweight for the cat's size. The less weight an animal carries, the faster it can go. Even the cheetah's skull is light compared to those of other cats its size.

Overall, cheetahs' bodies are smaller than those of the other large African cats, the leopard and the lion. A cheetah is usually between 6.5 and 8 feet long from its nose to the tip of its tail. (About a third of its length is tail!) A cheetah stands about 2.5 to 3 feet tall at the shoulder. Cheetahs weigh from 80 to 120 pounds, with males somewhat larger than females. A leopard can weigh up to 200 pounds, and a full-grown lion weighs up to 500 pounds.

How Big Is Big?

The largest members of the cat family are truly large. They range in size from about 6 feet to 12 feet long, measured from the tips of their noses to the tips of their tails. They weigh from 50 to 500 pounds, and are 22 to 40 inches tall at the shoulder.

Compared to other cats, the cheetah has a small head, slender build, and long legs and tail.

Cat	Length (ft.)	Weight (lbs.)	Height (in.)
Cheetah	6.5 – 8	80 – 120	30 – 36
Clouded Leopard	5.5 – 6.5	40 – 50	28 – 32
Cougar	8 – 9	80 – 220	24 – 30
Jaguar	5.5 – 9	220 – 350	28 – 32
Leopard	9.5 – 10	110 – 200	24 – 28
Lion	8 – 9	400 – 500	36 – 40
Snow Leopard	6 – 7	50 – 90	22 – 24
Tiger	10.5 – 12	350 – 500	36 – 39

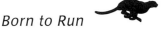

You might expect a runner to have long legs, and the cheetah does have long legs for a cat. But long legs are not the whole story when it comes to speed. Much of the cheetah's boost in speed comes from its very flexible spine. When a cheetah runs, its backbone flexes so much that its hind feet reach out ahead of its front feet. When the hind feet hit the ground, the cheetah stretches its back, pushes with its hind feet, and shoots through the air. At top speed, the cheetah can cover 20 feet in a single stride, even though its body is only about 4 feet long! Researchers estimate that the cheetah's flexible spine adds about 6 miles per hour to the cat's speed.

Digging In

Most cats, large and small, have retractile claws. When their paws are relaxed, their claws pull back into protective sheaths, or coverings. This helps keep the claws sharp. When the claws are needed to hunt, climb, or fight, the cats can extend them.

Cheetahs' claws retract fully when the cheetahs are cubs. After that, their claws are only partly retractile. Adult cheetahs can retract their claws only partway because their protective claw sheaths are too small to cover the claws completely. The cheetah's claws are always exposed. As the cat walks and runs, its claws rub on the ground, wear down, and become blunt like a dog's claws. The only exception is the cheetah's dewclaw, which is high up on the inside of the cat's wrist. The dewclaw does not come into contact with the ground, so it stays sharp.

Cheetahs are good climbers only when they are cubs and their claws are still sharp. Adult cheetahs do not climb well, although they can jump or scramble onto low branches of trees. But unlike most other cats, full-grown cheetahs do not depend on tree climbing to protect themselves from attack—they depend on speed. And cheetahs don't use their claws to catch and hold prey. Instead, they use their speed to outrun the prey and their teeth to hold and kill it. Blunt claws would be a disadvantage to other cats. But for cheetahs, blunt claws are an advantage. They help the cheetah run.

Fast Feet and a Tail to Steer

The cheetah's feet are like a built-in set of running shoes. When a cheetah runs, its doglike claws dig in and grip the ground. The cheetah spreads its toes wide to get better traction. The pads of the cheetah's feet are hard and tough with calluses. These pads grip the dirt, just as the rough surface of a running shoe sole grips the pavement. The tough pads also protect the cat's feet from sticks, stones, thorns, and heat. This protection is especially important to cheetahs that live in the Kalahari Desert in Africa. There the ground is rough, and the daytime temperature of the sand can reach 150°F.

Even the cheetah's long tail seems specially designed for fast movement. The bones of a cheetah's tail are flat, so the tail is shaped like a board standing on edge. Most animals use their tails for balance. But some researchers think a flat tail helps a cheetah make fast turns when chasing a dodging antelope. The tail acts like a boat's rudder. When the rudder is moved to one side, the water exerts pressure on that side of the rudder and pushes the back of the boat in the opposite direction. (If the rudder is moved to the right, the back of the boat moves to the left.) This makes the front of the boat swing in the same direction as the rudder. (If the rudder is moved to the right, the front of the boat swings to the right.) A cheetah running at

A cheetah swings its tail to the side to execute a fast turn.

high speed uses its tail in much the same way. The cat flicks its tail to one side when it wants to turn in that direction.

From nose to lungs to feet to tail, the cheetah is built to run. And it must run to live. To get the edge on the quick antelopes that are its main food, the cheetah has developed a hunting style all its own.

Chapter 3

Catching a Quick Meal

Cats are well known for using stealth to catch their prey and sharp claws to hold it. Most cats quietly creep close to their prey, then pounce or jump on it. Even large cats, such as lions, leopards, and jaguars, use this technique. But the cheetah has evolved to hunt fleet-footed antelopes. It depends on its speed, not its claws, to catch food.

The cheetah's fast-running prey live on the open savanna. The vast plains give the antelopes room to run, and they can see for long distances. With luck, the antelopes will spot any predator trying to sneak up on them.

Cheetahs also use the plains to their advantage. They have excellent eyesight and can see long distances across open land. A cheetah may scramble up onto a low branch of a solitary tree or climb a termite mound to get a better look across the plains. (Termite mounds in Africa can be almost 30 feet tall!) At other times, cheetahs amble slowly across the plains looking for antelopes. Some cheetahs simply sit and wait for their prey to walk by.

Thousands of antelopes of different kinds, including impalas, gazelles, bushbucks, and springboks, live in the central and southern parts of Africa. Cheetahs rarely have to travel a long distance to find something to eat. When prey is plentiful,

A cheetah stands in the branches of a tree, watching for distant prey.

cheetahs may have to walk only 2 to 3 miles per day to catch a quick meal. Even where prey is sparse, cheetahs usually range only 2.5 to 5 miles per day.

The size of antelope that a cheetah hunts depends on whether the cheetah is hunting by itself or with others. A single cheetah rarely hunts animals that weigh more than it does. Single cheetahs hunt small antelopes, such as Thomson's gazelles. But groups of two or three male cheetahs often go after larger

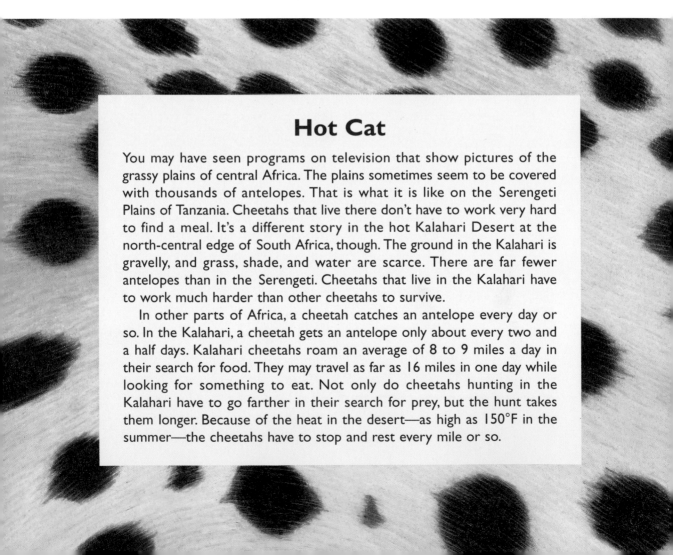

Hot Cat

You may have seen programs on television that show pictures of the grassy plains of central Africa. The plains sometimes seem to be covered with thousands of antelopes. That is what it is like on the Serengeti Plains of Tanzania. Cheetahs that live there don't have to work very hard to find a meal. It's a different story in the hot Kalahari Desert at the north-central edge of South Africa, though. The ground in the Kalahari is gravelly, and grass, shade, and water are scarce. There are far fewer antelopes than in the Serengeti. Cheetahs that live in the Kalahari have to work much harder than other cheetahs to survive.

In other parts of Africa, a cheetah catches an antelope every day or so. In the Kalahari, a cheetah gets an antelope only about every two and a half days. Kalahari cheetahs roam an average of 8 to 9 miles a day in their search for food. They may travel as far as 16 miles in one day while looking for something to eat. Not only do cheetahs hunting in the Kalahari have to go farther in their search for prey, but the hunt takes them longer. Because of the heat in the desert—as high as 150°F in the summer—the cheetahs have to stop and rest every mile or so.

antelopes, such as young wildebeest or hartebeest. (Female cheetahs with cubs do not seem to hunt these larger antelopes.) Adult male cheetahs can eat as much as 25 to 35 pounds of meat at one sitting, although they usually eat less. A Thomson's gazelle has only about 15 pounds of meat on it. This may be enough for one cheetah, but not for two or three. Males hunting together tend to go after larger antelopes so all of them have enough to eat. One researcher reported seeing a group of

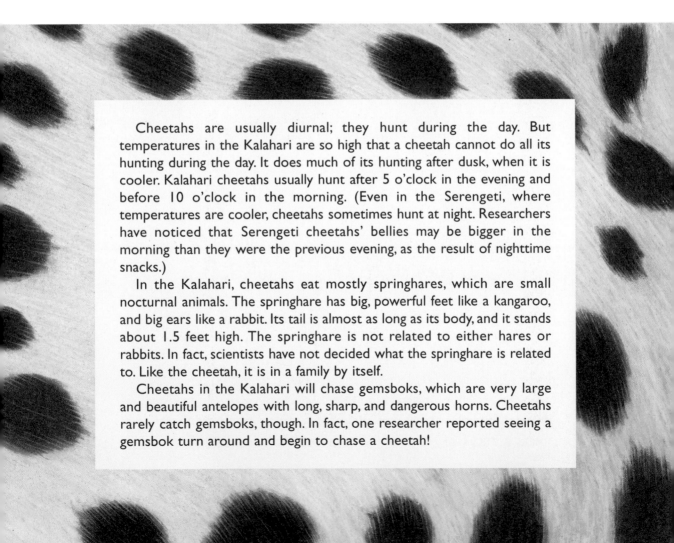

Cheetahs are usually diurnal; they hunt during the day. But temperatures in the Kalahari are so high that a cheetah cannot do all its hunting during the day. It does much of its hunting after dusk, when it is cooler. Kalahari cheetahs usually hunt after 5 o'clock in the evening and before 10 o'clock in the morning. (Even in the Serengeti, where temperatures are cooler, cheetahs sometimes hunt at night. Researchers have noticed that Serengeti cheetahs' bellies may be bigger in the morning than they were the previous evening, as the result of nighttime snacks.)

In the Kalahari, cheetahs eat mostly springhares, which are small nocturnal animals. The springhare has big, powerful feet like a kangaroo, and big ears like a rabbit. Its tail is almost as long as its body, and it stands about 1.5 feet high. The springhare is not related to either hares or rabbits. In fact, scientists have not decided what the springhare is related to. Like the cheetah, it is in a family by itself.

Cheetahs in the Kalahari will chase gemsboks, which are very large and beautiful antelopes with long, sharp, and dangerous horns. Cheetahs rarely catch gemsboks, though. In fact, one researcher reported seeing a gemsbok turn around and begin to chase a cheetah!

male cheetahs go right through a herd of gazelles while stalking a wildebeest!

Sometimes cheetahs hunt fully grown zebras, wildebeest, or hartebeest. Cheetahs have even been known to kill giraffe calves. But it is risky for the lightweight cheetah to attack large animals. Large prey have heavy hooves or sharp horns that can seriously injure or kill a cheetah.

Hungry cheetahs will not pass up small game, however. They hunt hares, or birds such as guinea fowl. Cheetahs, especially females, often walk from one clump of grass to another trying to scare up a hare or newborn gazelle that may be hiding there.

Cheetahs must hunt to eat. They rarely scavenge meat from other predators' kills. Cheetahs are timid, and usually there are other animals, such as hyenas or lions, at a carcass before a cheetah finds it. Cheetahs have relatively weak jaws and blunt claws, so they cannot fight the hyena, with its strong, crushing jaws, or the larger, heavier lion.

The Hunt

Although cheetahs can move very fast, they can run at top speed for only about a third of a mile. Before a cheetah begins to chase an antelope, it must get as close to the antelope as possible. If the cheetah is too far away when it begins the chase, it will not be able to catch its prey. Then the cheetah will have to start its hunt all over again.

Antelopes depend on their very sharp eyesight, more than on hearing or scent, to alert them to predators. A cheetah must approach an antelope herd cautiously so as not to frighten them. If a cheetah sees a herd of antelopes coming its way, it may wait until the herd is nearby, then run after one of the animals.

A cheetah's coloration helps it hide in dry grass.

Often, the cheetah will stalk the herd through long grass until it gets close enough to start its chase. As it creeps up on the antelopes, it takes advantage of any trees or shrubs that it can hide behind. If there is little cover, the cheetah may walk slowly toward the herd before making a run at it. A cheetah's spotted yellow coat provides camouflage as it carefully moves closer and closer to an antelope herd. The cheetah's coat blends in with the color of dry grass, and its spots resemble flickering shadows.

A cheetah charges into a herd of wildebeest to pick an animal to chase.

While it creeps up on the herd, the cheetah looks for an animal to chase. The cheetah chooses an antelope that is alone or one that is grazing at a distance from the main herd. Antelopes in high grass are good targets, because they don't notice an approaching cheetah right away. The cheetah also looks for antelopes that don't seem to be alert.

Once the cheetah gets as close as it can to the herd of antelopes, it does what seems to be a strange thing. After being so careful to keep the antelopes from seeing it, the cheetah suddenly sits up in plain sight of the grazing herd. This motion startles the antelopes, and they begin to run. The cheetah's action of showing itself to the antelopes is not really as strange as it seems. A running antelope, like a running human, can easily be knocked off balance. And that is what the cheetah does. It races up behind a fleeing antelope and slaps it with a paw to make it stumble.

One researcher noticed that there were sometimes small cuts on the flanks of antelopes that cheetahs had killed. He thought the cuts might have come from the cat's sharp dewclaws. But researchers are not yet sure whether or not a cheetah uses its dewclaws deliberately to catch and pull an antelope down.

The cheetah holds the antelope's throat for several minutes to be sure the animal is dead. The cheetah has worked hard for its meal. It cannot risk letting go of the antelope too soon. If the animal gets up and starts to run, the cheetah will probably be too exhausted to chase it a second time.

Knowing When to Quit

Antelopes have ways to avoid being eaten. They run fast, and they can dodge quickly to try to throw a cheetah off the track. But a cheetah is good at its job. On average, a cheetah catches one antelope every day or day and a half. When a cheetah chases adult prey, it succeeds in making a kill about half of the time. When chasing young animals, a cheetah rarely misses. The youngsters cannot run as fast as their parents. They also have less experience in escaping predators.

Part of the reason cheetahs are such successful hunters is that they know when to quit. Running at 70 miles an hour, or even 40 miles an hour, takes a great deal of energy. A cheetah tends to stop chasing an antelope when the energy it will have to put out to catch the animal is greater than the energy it will get from the meat.

Of course, cheetahs don't think this all out. They learn it by watching their mother and through their own hunting

experiences. They learn that they get full and have more energy if they eat antelopes rather than hares. Cheetahs also learn that their energy comes back faster after short runs than after long ones. They don't have to rest as long between chases, so they can make more chases in a day. More chases mean a better chance of catching a quick bite.

If a cheetah tried as hard as it could to catch every animal it chased, it might soon become so exhausted it could no longer hunt at all. This is why cheetahs often give up the chase if their prey turns too quickly and dodges off in a different direction. They simply stop, rest, and then find another animal to chase. Once a cheetah does stop a chase, it must rest for as long as an hour before it has enough energy to hunt again.

A cheetah rests as it strangles a Thomson's gazelle.

Taking Time Out

Once the prey is dead, the cheetah drags it away to a shady spot, if it can find one. If there is no shade, the cat tries to find some kind of cover, such as a bush or a clump of tall grass, where other animals cannot see it. In the harsh Kalahari Desert, where there is little cover, cheetahs still drag their prey away from the site of the kill, even if it's only a few feet.

After the hunt, the cheetah is exhausted. It is breathing so hard that it must rest for 5 to 10 minutes before it can eat. Sometimes the cat may need as much as half an hour to catch its breath before it can begin to feed. Once it has rested, the cheetah quickly eats as much of its hard-won meal as it can.

The cheetah may not get to eat all the meat from its prey. Soaring vultures soon notice the carcass and circle overhead to wait their turn to eat. Other predators see the vultures and know that an animal has died. Lions, hyenas, or jackals may move in to try to take away the cheetah's meal.

One out of every 10 antelopes a cheetah catches is stolen by bolder animals. One researcher watched a female cheetah kill a gazelle, which was immediately stolen by a hyena. The cheetah caught another gazelle only 50 feet away. The hyena took that meal, too! A cheetah can usually protect its kill from smaller predators, such as jackals. But even jackals can sometimes harass a cheetah into giving up its meal. Other more surprising scavengers can keep a cheetah from eating. Although it was an unusual case, biologist George Schaller reported that he once saw a cheetah chased away from its prey by a flock of very determined vultures!

A trio of cheetahs perches atop a termite mound.

Chapter 4

Lifestyles of the Swift and Famous

When it comes to hunting styles, cheetahs are unique among cats. But they are also unique in the way they live and get along with each other. Most kinds of cats are either solitary (living alone), or social (living in groups). Nearly all cats, including most of the large cats, are solitary. Lions are social cats. They live in prides, which are groups of males, females, and cubs. Cheetahs are the only cats that are both solitary and social. Some cheetahs live alone. Some live with other cheetahs. Perhaps cheetahs as a group are best described as "sort of solitary."

Sort of Solitary

Female and male cheetahs have different lifestyles. A female cheetah lives alone except when she has cubs. She keeps company with male cheetahs only when she is in estrus—ready to mate.

Female cheetahs establish large home ranges. A home range is the area a cheetah regularly covers in search of food, water, and mates. Home ranges are not defended against intruders. In fact, cheetahs' home ranges often overlap. In the Serengeti National Park in Tanzania, the home range of a female cheetah covers up to 300 square miles. Females have large home ranges in the Serengeti because they follow the migration of the Thomson's gazelles. The gazelles move as the supply of grass and water on the plains changes. Female cheetahs stay close to the antelopes so that they have enough food to feed themselves and their cubs.

A female cheetah's home range may overlap those of her mother, sisters, and daughters. Young females learn from their mother where to find water and lots of prey. They learn where there are few predators and where there are good places to hide cubs. This knowledge will help the females—and their cubs—to survive.

If an area is good for raising cubs, unrelated female cheetahs are sure to have their home ranges there as well. There is little friction between females, however. Female cheetahs, even related ones, avoid each other. If two female cheetahs spot each other, they may immediately head off in different directions. Sometimes they sit and stare at each other from as far as a mile away. Finally, one will walk off.

The social behavior of male cheetahs is more complex than that of females. While some males live alone, others live in groups. Male littermates usually stay together for life, forming a coalition or alliance. A coalition is a small group of animals that help each other get food or defend territory. Male groups are rare among cats. Lions are the only other cat species whose males—again usually brothers—live together in groups.

Seventy percent of all cheetah coalitions are made up only of brothers. Pairs of male cheetahs are almost always brothers. Rarely do two unrelated, single male cheetahs join together. Trios, however, usually consist of two brothers and one unrelated male.

A male who has no male littermates travels alone.

Sometimes, however, a lone male tries to join a coalition of brothers. He is likely to be chased away. If he stays nearby, he may be attacked and severely bitten or even killed. Even if he is accepted by the coalition, the brothers may continue to be aggressive toward him. They may slap or hiss at him if he tries to groom their fur. During play, they may bite him. The brothers may lie very close to each other, grooming each other's fur and purring, and refuse to let the single cheetah come near. The single cheetah may end up lying in the sun while the brothers lie in the only spot of shade. It may take several years for a coalition to fully accept a new partner.

Why do single male cheetahs risk being killed to join a coalition? Why do they put up with constant aggression once they're in a group? It is probably because a coalition can better defend a territory.

It's My Turf

Male cheetahs fall into two groups. The first group is made up of solitary adult males, as well as pairs or trios of young brothers that have not yet reached their full weight and sexual maturity. These single or immature males, sometimes called nomads, travel over huge home ranges of up to 700 square miles. Nomads' ranges overlap the ranges of females and other nomads. In fact, young male cheetahs may stay in their mother's home range until they are fully grown. Then they strike out on their own.

Like female cheetahs, nomadic males appear to follow the migrating Thomson's gazelles. But it is more likely that the nomads follow the females that are following the gazelles. Nomadic males try to stay close to females so that they can mate when the females come into estrus. But by following the females, nomadic males risk coming into conflict with another group of male cheetahs: territorial males.

All territorial males are adults that have reached sexual maturity, and most are members of coalitions. These males stake out territories that measure about 12 square miles—much smaller than the huge home ranges of females and nomadic males. Territorial male cheetahs actively defend their territories against other males.

Male cheetahs mark the edges of their territories by spraying urine on shrubs, trees, and clumps of grass. They leave feces on high landmarks, such as fallen trees and termite mounds. Leaving a scent mark on a high spot increases the chance that other cheetahs will find the mark. Scent marks warn other cheetahs that an area is occupied, and that intruders may be killed. Cheetahs heed the scent marks. One researcher saw two territorial males check a scent mark left by males in a neighboring territory. The two males immediately turned and ran away.

Territorial cheetahs do not follow the gazelles or the female cheetahs on their migration. Instead, they claim areas that provide shade for resting and enough trees and shrubs to hide hunting cheetahs. Territories usually have a source of water and plenty of prey. These are just the kinds of places where female cheetahs tend to hunt and raise their cubs. So territorial males simply wait for females to come into their territory, and then they try to mate with the females.

When females enter a male territory, nomadic males may follow them. This can be very dangerous for the nomads. The nomads—who are usually alone—are outnumbered by the coalition controlling the territory. Territorial males will not hesitate to fight a single male. Researchers have rarely seen fights between cheetahs, but most of the fights they have seen have been between coalitions and single cheetahs. One researcher saw a coalition of three cheetahs chase and catch a single male. They bit him, held him down, and strangled him the way they would kill prey.

Cheetah coalitions may move into an unoccupied territory, or take one away from a smaller coalition. The larger the coalition, the longer it can hold a territory. This may be why a pair of cheetahs eventually takes a new member into their group. Coalitions of males tend to fight other cheetahs only when the other group has fewer cheetahs in it—trios may attack pairs or loners, for example. A coalition may not even approach a female if she has several large, adolescent cubs with her.

Males in a coalition may have a better chance of mating with females than single males do. Breeding programs at zoos have shown that female cheetahs can be picky about the mates they choose. If a female has several males to choose from, she may pick one to mate with. A coalition may surround a lone female and keep her from running off until she mates with one of them. If there's only one male, the female may be able to get away if she doesn't want to mate.

Cheetahs: The Next Generation

Scientists who watch cheetahs have a hard time knowing when a female is in estrus. During estrus, the female may rub her head on the ground, twitch her tail, or call out more often than usual. She is likely to roll on the ground if a male is nearby. Some biologists have noticed that when a female is in estrus, she urinates and defecates more often than usual. These researchers say that a female in estrus tends to leave her scent on high places, similar to the way males mark territories. The

A male cheetah approaches a female in an attempt to mate with her.

scientists believe that hormones in a female's urine and feces tell males when she is ready to mate.

For two or three weeks before a female cheetah comes into estrus, male cheetahs may try to come close to her to sniff her or the grass she has been sitting on. Males may growl or hiss at each other when she is around. They may slap the female and knock her down if she tries to run away, although they do not bite her. The female often slaps them back and growls.

Scientists have seldom seen wild cheetahs mate. This may be because males and females spend so little time mating—a few minutes to no more than three days—that scientists may just miss it. Or it may be that cheetahs mate primarily at night. Regardless of the reason, little is known about what goes on immediately before and after mating.

During one cheetah study, a group of biologists saw two cheetahs mate in broad daylight. They saw a female, whom they had named Solitaire, urinate frequently—about every 10 minutes. A male they had named Paka came across her scent marks. He began yipping and purring and rapidly following her scent. When she heard him calling, Solitaire ran toward him and they quickly mated. Afterward, she rolled on the ground and seemed to ignore Paka.

Over the next two days, Paka stayed very close to Solitaire. Every time she moved, he followed, sometimes growling and hissing. Sometimes she hissed when he got too close, and other times she slapped at him. On the afternoon of the second day, while Paka slept, Solitaire left. "In slow motion...she carefully got to her feet...[and] step by careful step she crept off," wrote the researchers. Alone again on the vast plains, Solitaire, like other female cheetahs, would raise and provide for her cubs by herself.

A young cheetah cub follows its mother across the savanna.

Chapter 5

Mother on the Run

A cheetah mother is pregnant for 90 to 95 days. At the end of that time, she finds a lair, a quiet, safe place to have her cubs. She usually chooses a marshy area, tall grass, or a spot on a rocky hillside in which to hide her babies. She leaves them there while she hunts.

Cheetahs usually have three or four cubs in each litter, although they may have as many as eight. Newborn cheetah cubs weigh only 8 to 12 ounces, and they are helpless. The cubs open their eyes for the first time 2 to 8 days after birth. They begin crawling at about one week and walk when they are 10 to 11 days old.

A very young cheetah cub has dark grayish fur, with faint spots on its belly. On its back, it has a light-colored mane or mantle. This is a cloaklike covering of long hair that grows from its neck to the base of its tail.

Cheetah cubs' coloration may help protect them from predators. Some biologists think that from a distance a cub could be mistaken for a honey badger, which is a bad-tempered, aggressive animal. Predators that mistake a cheetah cub for a honey badger may avoid the cub rather than attack it. Other biologists disagree with the honey-badger theory. They think that the cubs' coloring simply makes them somewhat harder to see. The light mane blends in with the light-colored grass, and the dark belly fur looks like shadows or soil under the grass.

Babies at Risk

A mother cheetah may stay with her cubs for a day or two after they are born. But she cannot stay with them constantly. She must continue to hunt for food for herself, so she can produce milk to feed them.

Female cheetahs that don't have cubs often hunt small game, such as hares or newborn gazelles. But because it takes a lot of energy to produce milk for hungry cubs, mothers must hunt adult antelopes. And because adult antelopes are more difficult to catch than newborns, mother cheetahs spend more time hunting than do females without cubs.

One reason the hunts take longer is that mother cheetahs often fall asleep while following their prey. Young cubs are so demanding that their mother gets little rest while they are around. They play on her, and they want to nurse often. So when she's away from them, she may take the opportunity to have a short nap. But if she does, the antelope herd she's following may wander away. Then she must catch up to the herd again.

A mother cheetah leaves her cubs hidden in the lair while she hunts. When she returns, she chirps to call them. They run out of hiding and come to her. She lies down on her side so the cubs can drink her milk. After the cubs have nursed, she cleans them with her tongue and purrs.

A mother cheetah may move her cubs to a new lair as often as every day or two. She may do this to prevent the cubs' scent from building up in the lair, which would make it easier for predators to find the cubs. One researcher watched a cheetah move her cubs 20 times.

The mother cheetah can carry only one cub in her mouth at a time. So she may have to make several trips from the old lair

Purr-fect Contentment

Humans usually think of a purring cat as a happy cat. Domestic cats purr when you pet them. And cheetahs that have been raised by humans purr when someone scratches their chin.

Kittens first purr when they are about one week old. They probably learn to purr from their mothers. When cats are very young, the sound of purring is closely associated with food. Female cats (including cheetahs) purr while they nurse their litters. The kittens (and cubs) purr while nursing, too! The sound of their mother's purr, as well as the vibration caused by the purring, may help very young, still-blind kittens find their mother when it is time to eat. The sound of a purring kitten may also let the other kittens in the litter know when it's time to nurse. If one kitten starts nursing—and purring—the others in the litter soon rush to their mother's side.

There are reports, however, that cats have been known to purr when they are in pain or distress. Cats have even been reported to purr when they are dying. How does this fit in with our image of the contented, purring cat?

Purring is primarily a social sound. Cats purr when they are interacting peacefully with each other—or with humans. Researchers have often reported hearing cheetahs purr while the cats are grooming each other. Some think that purring in times of stress may be the cat's way of asking for social contact in the form of petting or grooming. Zoo vets who work frequently with cheetahs, however, say that they have never heard a sick, hurt, or dying cheetah purr.

to the new one. Once she has moved all of the cubs, she may go back to the old hiding place several times. She may do this to make sure she has left no one behind.

Despite the mother cheetah's precautions, it is unlikely that all of her cubs will survive. Almost 70 percent of infant cheetahs die before they are eight weeks old, the age at which cubs leave the lair to travel with their mother. (One study in the Serengeti showed that out of 125 cubs born, only 36 lived to leave the lair.) Cubs may die of exposure—from too much sun or from rain that soaks and chills them. Grass fires kill some cubs. Some starve if their mother stays away too long on a hunt, or if she is hurt or killed. Other cubs die of disease. Still others are killed by lions or hyenas that find the lair.

After the cubs leave the lair and start traveling with their mother, they are still at risk. They may not quickly recognize danger, such as the approach of a lion or leopard. Even if the cubs scatter and hide, as their mother tries to drive the predator away, the lion or leopard may circle around to get the cubs. Natural disasters such as floods can kill cubs. Some are even hit by cars. Another 20 percent of all cheetah cubs die between two and four months old. (In the Serengeti study mentioned above, hazards such as these took the lives of 24 of the 125 cubs.)

By the time they are four months old, the cubs are fast enough to outrun most predators. Even so, another 5 percent die before they separate from their mother at 15 to 18 months. A total of 95 percent of cheetah cubs die before they leave their mothers. (In the Serengeti study, only 7 of the 125 cubs studied lived long enough to go out on their own.) If a mother cheetah loses all her cubs, she will be ready to mate again within a few weeks.

Will You Be My Mother?

While most cubs die if their mother is killed or hurt and cannot return to the lair, some cubs manage to beat the odds against them. They survive by being adopted by other cheetahs. The cheetahs that adopt orphaned cubs are usually mothers with cubs of their own. However, orphans may also be adopted by male coalitions.

Raising a cheetah cub to adulthood is difficult. Even in zoos, almost 30 percent of cheetah cubs die before they are six months old.

Cheetah cubs that attach themselves to other groups are usually at least six months old. At that age, they are no longer nursing. They are able to scavenge meat from their adopted family's kill. Although this takes food away from the family's cubs, it is not usually enough to weaken or starve them. A mother cheetah rarely chases a young orphan away, although she may hiss at it.

A cheetah and her cubs chase one another. When cubs play, they learn skills that they will use in the hunt.

Orphans may stay with their new families anywhere from a few days to a year. Sometimes they become separated from their first adopted family and must find a second one. When they are old enough, the cubs go their own way. Male cubs that are adopted by a male coalition, however, may stay with the pair and become part of the coalition.

Following Mom

When cheetah cubs are about eight weeks old, they begin to follow their mother as she looks for prey. For the first few months, she hides them in tall grass or under a bush whenever she is hunting. They stay there until she comes back with the kill.

Although the cubs are still nursing, their mother starts introducing them to meat. They don't always like it at first. They may sniff the meat and back away from the strange smell. But when their mother calls them, they come back. Some cubs continue to nurse even when their siblings are eating meat. As they get older, however, their mother weans them—she nurses them less often, until finally they are eating only meat.

Cheetah cubs are very playful. They run around, climb a few feet into trees and bushes, and jump back down. They chase each other, stalk and pounce on each other, and slap each other. They may just be having fun. But many researchers think that playing teaches young animals some of the skills they will need as adults.

As the cubs get older, their fur gets lighter in color and their spots become more distinct. Their mantle gets shorter, although it may not disappear completely—many adult cheetahs have a very short remnant of the mane. The cubs' claws outgrow their claw sheaths. They can no longer retract their claws completely.

By about four and a half to five months, when the cubs are able to outrun predators, their coloration is similar to an adult's. They are ready to begin hunting.

Hunting School

Although ancient peoples tamed cheetahs, they never trained the cats to hunt. Nor do cheetahs instinctively know how to hunt. A cheetah must learn to hunt from its mother. That is one reason why all the cheetahs people used for hunting had to be taken from the wild as adults.

To start the cubs' hunting lessons, their mother may bring them a small antelope she has caught but not killed. She may knock the antelope down and let it get up again. The cubs may chase the antelope and slap at it. But they may be frightened by the strange animal. Their mother may have to catch it again before it gets away. Or the cubs may lose their meal altogether. But they catch on quickly. Between the ages of five and seven months, the cubs begin to knock down and strangle prey by themselves.

When a mother cheetah first takes her cubs hunting, they don't understand the process. They may get in their mother's way or walk toward the prey before they are close enough to catch it. They may scare the gazelles away. Cubs may chase an antelope without trying to slap it, or give up the chase before they get close enough. Sometimes young cheetahs sit and call the prey with a yip, the way they call members of their family to them!

Learning what to chase and what not to chase takes a while. Cubs may chase birds, which escape by taking to the air. They may chase jackals or lizards. They may stalk prey that is much too large for them, such as a giraffe or a rhinoceros. Over time, the cubs learn how to hunt and what to hunt. But they still leave much of the hunting to their mother.

Cheetah cubs grow fast. By six months, they are half the size of their mother. At a year, they may be almost as big as she is. When her cubs are between 10 and 15 months old, the female cheetah is ready to mate again.

A six-month-old cub carries a young Thomson's gazelle. Young cheetahs hunt small prey as they perfect their skills.

Going Out on Their Own

When the cubs are 15 to 18 months old, the cheetah family breaks up. Scientists are not sure if the mother leaves the cubs or the cubs leave their mother. They think it is most likely that the mother walks away from her cubs. Even though the cubs may be as large as their mother, she is still doing most of the hunting—and getting only a small part of the food. In addition, the mother may already have mated, so she could soon begin raising a new litter of cubs.

The break in the family may be quite sudden. One day their mother is with the cubs, and the next day the family has separated. The family may split up and come back together a few times before the break is final.

The cubs stay together for up to six months. Inexperienced cubs traveling in a group are safer from predators, and they have the benefit of hunting together. Although they are not expert hunters, there is a good chance that one of them will manage to catch something to eat. Young cheetahs tend to stay within their mother's home range until they are at least two years old. It is the area they know best. It is easier for them to find food, water, and shelter there.

At about 22 months, the young females come into estrus for the first time and are ready to have cubs of their own. They go off by themselves and establish home ranges within or overlapping their mother's range.

When they are two to three years old, the males reach sexual maturity and leave their mother's home range. At first, they are nomadic. They are too young and inexperienced to establish their own territory or take one over from other male cheetahs.

As young cheetahs grow to adulthood, they face many dangers—predators, disease, starvation. But cheetahs that survive

Young cheetahs may have a hard time finding food after they leave their mother. These very hungry cheetahs are watching for prey.

to become adults have other problems—problems that threaten the survival of their species. Some of these problems can be traced back thousands of years, to a time when most of the world's cheetahs died.

Chapter 6

Cheetahs in a Bottleneck

Some scientists think that *Acinonyx jubatus* almost died out 20,000 years ago during the last ice age, when all the other species of cheetahs became extinct. When most of the animals in a species die, leaving only a small number, scientists say the species is going through a "population bottleneck."

When a species goes through a population bottleneck, the number of individuals that are left alive may be very small. For example, in the 1980s, the population of wild California condors decreased to only six birds. No one knows how many common cheetahs were left when all the other species of cheetahs died off.

A population bottleneck may result from a disease that kills most of the animals of a species. Bottlenecks may also occur if the climate changes, becoming too hot or cold, too wet or dry for the species. Perhaps the food a species eats dies off for some reason. When a species' food source is gone, the species dies too if it cannot eat something else. The world's climate became much colder during the ice age. Perhaps the other kinds of cheetahs, or their prey animals, were unable to adapt to the new conditions. As a result, all of the cheetah species except *Acinonyx jubatus* became extinct.

During the last ice age, the world's population of common cheetahs dropped very low.

Adapting to Change

Over thousands of years, the environment changes. Regions become hotter or colder, wetter or drier. Species of plants and animals may die, survive, or flourish depending on how readily they can adapt when the environment changes. The ability to adapt depends on many factors.

Animals that are highly specialized can live in only one kind of place or eat one kind of food. They are likely to die if the environment changes. Koalas, for example, eat only eucalyptus leaves. If a change in climate killed all the eucalyptus trees, the koalas would probably become extinct, too.

The adaptability of a species also depends on the variety of physical traits present among individuals in the species. Among cheetahs, for example, some cats may be a little faster or slower, bigger or smaller, have thicker or thinner fur, or have longer or shorter tails. While the environment is stable, these differences may not affect the cheetahs' survival. But let's imagine the grassland gradually changed to woodland, where the cheetahs could not use their speed to hunt. Those little differences might add up to big changes over time.

It might turn out that slower, smaller cats with shorter tails could maneuver better in the trees than faster cats could. Because they might be better able to hunt in the new environment, the slow cats could have a better chance of surviving to have cubs. Some of the slower cheetahs' cubs would probably be slow and small, with shorter tails. Larger, faster cats, unable to hunt in the woods, would starve. The speed demon cat of the plains could gradually disappear.

Scientists have seen this kind of adaptation in the Galápagos Islands, near Ecuador. As the climate alternately becomes wetter and drier, different kinds of plants flourish. In dry weather, plants with tough, spiny seeds increase in number. Plants with small seeds survive better when it's wet.

In the Galápagos there are many kinds of finches. Some have large, heavy beaks, and others have small beaks. Scientists noticed that during drought, heavy-beaked finches grew in number. They could break open and eat tough seeds, but finches with smaller beaks couldn't. Because they could not survive as well, the numbers of small-beaked finches declined. When the weather got wet again, the number of plants producing small seeds increased, and so did the number of small-beaked finches.

Genes: A Blueprint for Life

Although individual animals may survive a population bottleneck, their species as a whole may develop problems. One set of problems results from inbreeding. When there are very few animals of a species left, closely related individuals, such as siblings or cousins, are more likely to mate with each other. Eventually, all the individuals in a species may have very similar traits because they have very similar sets of genes.

Genes are found in the cells of every living thing. They contain the instructions that help determine what an organism looks like and how it works. Genes control an animal's physical traits, such as eye color or coat pattern. They affect the size of a cheetah's lungs, the slenderness of its bones, how its respiratory system works, and, therefore, how fast it can run. Genes also control an animal's ability to resist disease or to adapt to changes in the environment.

The instructions in genes are coded in DNA (deoxyribonucleic acid). DNA is a complex molecule shaped like a twisting ladder. DNA tells cells which proteins to build. The proteins may end up as part of bone, blood, hair, organ, or disease-fighting cells, or as enzymes that cause chemical reactions in other cells.

Cheetahs and other mammals each have about 100,000 genes. The genes work in pairs. A pair of genes controls every trait, such as coat pattern. An individual's genes are gathered together into long chains called chromosomes. Most cells contain a complete set of chromosomes, although only a few genes may be "switched on" and working in any particular cell. For example, there is no need for a liver cell to know how to make bone, so the genes coding for bone production are "switched off" in liver cells.

The only cells that do not have a full set of chromosomes are sperm and egg cells. These cells carry only one-half of an individual's chromosomes and contain only one gene for each trait. When sperm and egg cells merge together at mating, the new embryo inherits a full set of chromosomes—half from its mother, and half from its father.

Genetic Diversity Is the Spice of Life

Among all the individuals in a species there may be several varieties of each gene. Varieties of genes are called alleles. In humans, for example, one gene determines blood type, but there are three different blood-type alleles: A, B, and O. Domestic cats have a set of genes that determine their coat pattern and color. Cats can have splotched, striped, or solid-colored coats, depending on the combination of coat-pattern alleles in their chromosomes.

No matter how many alleles of a gene there are in a population, each individual has exactly two. Although there are three human blood-type alleles, for example, humans inherit only two blood-type alleles from their parents—an A, B, or O from their mother, and an A, B, or O from their father.

When a population of a species has many different alleles, scientists say that the population is genetically diverse or that it has a lot of genetic diversity. Genetic diversity can mean the difference between survival and extinction when an animal's environment changes. But what happens when only a few animals survive the changes?

When most of the animals in a population die off, as may have happened to cheetahs during the last ice age, there may be many alleles that are not passed on to young animals. The species becomes less genetically diverse. As the variety of alleles decreases, certain valuable traits may disappear from the population. The species may become less able to adapt to changes in the environment.

If genes controlled only traits such as coat pattern and eye color, a decrease in genetic diversity might not be a problem for cheetahs—or any other animal. But genes also control life-and-death characteristics, such as a cheetah's ability to resist disease.

A Cheetah is a Cheetah is a Cheetah

Animals depend on their immune system to protect them from disease. Their immune system depends on millions of immunoglobulins, or antibodies.

Immunoglobulins are proteins in the blood that scan the blood for invaders, such as viruses or bacteria. They can tell the difference between foreign particles and the cells that are part of the animal. When they recognize a foreign particle in the blood, the immunoglobulins tell their cells to begin dividing. They make millions more antibodies that attack the viruses or bacteria and destroy them. The antibodies attack only foreign cells and leave the animal's own cells alone.

Because their job is to recognize foreign tissue and destroy it, antibodies attack organs that are transplanted from one animal to another. When this happens, we say that the animal has "rejected" the organ transplant. Rejection can be a problem when an organ such as a kidney or heart is transplanted from one human to another. To prevent rejection, doctors give a patient drugs to suppress the immune system so that it will not attack the new organ.

Suppression of the immune system would not be necessary

Yipes! Stripes!

Most cheetahs have the familiar yellow coat with dark brown spots. But king cheetahs look very different. A king cheetah's cream-colored fur is covered with large, irregularly shaped splotches. Along its back, from the nape of its neck to the base of its tail, are three dark, broad stripes.

The first king cheetah was sighted in Zimbabwe in 1926 by Major A. L. Cooper. So the king was first named "Cooper's cheetah." Some people thought it was the offspring of a cheetah and a leopard. Reginald I. Pocock of the British Museum raved about the newly discovered cat. He called it "the handsomest member of the cat tribe," and named it *Acinonyx rex,* the king cheetah.

Mystery Cat

For 55 years after Cooper's report, the king cheetah was almost a myth. During that time, there were only 11 dependable sightings of live king cheetahs. Only 13 king cheetah skins were known to exist. Up until the 1980s, kings had been seen only in Zimbabwe, Botswana, and the Transvaal region of South Africa.

So the striped and splotched cub born to a common cheetah at the Cheetah Research and Breeding Center in De Wildt, South Africa, in the spring of 1981 was a complete surprise. Two days later, a pregnant common cheetah De Wildt had sent to the zoo in Port Elizabeth, South Africa, also gave birth to a king cub. The zoo returned the striped cub to De Wildt, which has the largest captive population of king cheetahs in the world.

Although Pocock gave the cat a name of its own, the king cheetah is not a new cheetah species. Its beautiful coat pattern is simply a color variation of the common cheetah pattern. Other spotted cats also exhibit coat color variations. Two well-known examples are the black leopard and the black jaguar.

A king cheetah's distinctive coat pattern is a combination of stripes and splotches.

Special Genes

In the wild, king cheetahs are extremely rare. This is partly due to the way the king coat pattern gene is passed on from parent to offspring.

A cheetah's coat pattern, like all its physical traits, is controlled by a pair of genes. Most cheetahs' genes give them the common cheetah coat pattern. But in some cheetah populations, there are cats that have a different coat pattern allele in their cells—the king cheetah allele.

Although every trait is controlled by a pair of genes, one allele may be dominant and one may be recessive. If a dominant and a recessive allele are in a cell together, the dominant allele determines what trait shows up in the animal. The recessive trait remains hidden, although it is still there. The animal can pass the recessive trait on to its offspring. Because the animal "carries" the recessive allele in its cells, it is called a carrier.

The spotted coat pattern of common cheetahs is caused by a dominant gene. The king coat pattern is a recessive trait. For a cheetah cub to have a king coat, both of its parents must carry the recessive king gene, and the cub must inherit it from both of them. If its parents are both king cheetahs, the cub is a king. If one parent is a king cheetah and the other is a carrier of the king gene, the cub has a 50 percent chance of being a king. There is only a 25 percent chance that a cub will be a king if both of its parents are carriers of the king gene. A cheetah that inherits one common gene and one king gene is a common cheetah. But it still carries the king gene in its cells and may pass that gene on to its cubs.

Since approximately 95 percent of all cheetah cubs die before separating from their mother, there is only a small chance that a king cub will live to be an adult and pass on its special genes. Even if the king does live long enough to mate, it may never mate with another cheetah that has the king gene. Then all its cubs will be common cheetahs, although some may inherit the king gene.

To preserve this rare color variation, more zoos are raising king cheetahs. The De Wildt center sent the first king cheetah out of Africa to the Cincinnati Zoo in 1989. By 1995, the Cincinnati Zoo, the St. Louis Zoo, the Caldwell Zoo (in Tyler, Texas) and the San Diego Wild Animal Park all had king cheetahs.

when transplanting an organ between cheetahs. Scientists learned this by making skin grafts—a very small kind of organ transplant—between seven pairs of cheetahs. First they grafted a small patch of skin from a domestic cat onto each cheetah. Within 12 days, the cheetahs' bodies had rejected the grafts. That proved to the scientists that the cheetahs' immune systems were working the way they were supposed to. The antibodies were able to recognize foreign tissue.

Then the scientists took a small piece of skin from each cheetah and grafted it back onto the same cheetah. The graft healed just like a cut on the cheetah would heal. The researchers had not expected the immune system to attack the graft, because the skin was not foreign tissue.

Finally, the scientists grafted small patches of skin from one cheetah to another. In most other species of animals, these grafts would have been rejected, just as organ transplants in humans are rejected. But the cheetahs' skin grafts healed perfectly! The cheetahs' immune systems had not recognized the skin of another cheetah as being foreign tissue. Each cheetah's body had accepted the skin of another cheetah as if the graft were its own skin. This experiment proved that the cheetahs' immunity genes were almost identical.

Unhealthy Inheritance

If a population of animals has many alleles for immunity, or disease resistance, the animals are unlikely to all get sick from the same disease. Even if a disease kills some of the animals, others will probably survive. The disease may make the survivors only slightly sick, or it may not bother them at all. In addition, the survivors' offspring may inherit the genes that made their parents immune to that particular disease. But if all the animals in a population have very similar disease immunity genes, a disease that makes one animal sick could very well make all of them sick. If the disease is deadly, then all the animals, or a very large number of them, could die.

Scientists have discovered that all cheetahs—no matter where in Africa they live—have sets of alleles that are very much alike. The similarity is especially great in the clusters of genes that control the cheetahs' resistance to disease. In most species, the combination of alleles in these immunity clusters is so different from animal to animal that the chance of finding two animals with the same combination is very small. But among cheetahs, there is little variation in the immunity clusters. As a result, if a group of cheetahs is exposed to a deadly disease, many of them could die.

In 1982, a disease called feline infectious peritonitis (FIP) broke out among the cheetahs living at Wildlife Safari, a wild animal park in Oregon. House cats can catch FIP, too, but only 5 percent of house cats that become infected with FIP die. The rest recover. In the animal park, however, 50 percent of the cheetahs died from FIP.

Lack of genetic diversity may be the cause of another problem for cheetahs. Male cheetahs have a high percentage of abnormal sperm cells. In most animal species, if 20 percent of a male's sperm are abnormal, the animal is infertile. Although the male may mate with a female, she will not become pregnant. It is common for 70 percent of a male cheetah's sperm to be abnormal. Yet cheetahs in the wild manage to keep having cubs. Scientists are not yet sure that sperm abnormality results from the cheetah's low genetic diversity. There may be other reasons why male cheetahs have high numbers of abnormal sperm.

Hunting to Extinction

Disease and environmental changes are not the only causes of population bottlenecks. Overhunting by humans is another cause. Until the middle of the twentieth century, humans commonly hunted cheetahs for their spotted skins. Overhunting may have reduced cheetah numbers enough to cause a second population bottleneck. Two population bottlenecks in the history of the species could explain the cheetah's extreme lack of genetic diversity.

Considering that cheetahs may twice have almost become extinct, that they are vulnerable to disease because of their lack of genetic diversity, and that they are often infertile, it is a wonder that cheetahs still exist. And there are even more pressures in the wild that threaten the cheetah's survival.

Cheetahs on the Run

In much of its range, *Acinonyx jubatus* is an endangered species. It is estimated that only 9,000 to 12,000 cheetahs are left in the wild. Cheetahs disappeared from India in the 1940s. They probably died out in the Middle East sometime in the 1970s, although some researchers think a few cheetahs may still live in Iran or Afghanistan.

In the past, humans hunted the beautiful runners for their spotted coats. They made clothes, belts, hats, handbags, and rugs from the hides. Since then, many countries have forbidden the import of cheetah skins unless the hunter has a legal hunting permit. South Africa, Namibia, Botswana, and Zimbabwe allow a certain number of cheetahs to be hunted each year. The money the governments earn from hunting permit fees helps to support wildlife conservation programs.

Other cheetahs are killed by farmers. As the number of people in Africa has increased, so has the number of farms and ranches. Young cattle are just the right size for cheetahs to hunt. Many governments allow farmers to protect their livestock by shooting cheetahs that are considered pests.

Farmers and ranchers put up fences to protect crops and keep their cattle together. But fences are deadly to cheetahs. When they run at high speed, cheetahs don't see the wire in the fences. A cheetah that runs at full speed into wire or a fencepost is likely to be killed instantly. Even if the cheetah lives through the crash, it has little chance for survival. A cheetah with broken bones or other injuries cannot hunt or avoid predators. It soon starves to death, or it is killed by hyenas or lions.

Farming takes away the grassland that antelopes and cheetahs need for survival. In addition, humans hunt antelopes for food. Fewer antelopes mean less food for cheetahs. As the grasslands and antelopes disappear, so do the cheetahs.

Even in national parks and wild animal preserves where cheetahs are protected, the cats face serious threats. The parks don't protect only cheetahs. They also protect an enemy of the cheetah, the lion. Some parks contain 10 times as many lions as cheetahs. In those parks, it sometimes seems that cheetah cubs are the lions' favorite snack. In places where hyena and lion numbers are high, cheetahs are scarce.

Even people who love cheetahs can hurt them. Visitors to game parks often watch cheetahs from buses. The buses can disturb a cheetah's hunt or, if a cheetah is very timid, drive it away from a kill. The amount of interference caused by tourist buses depends on the skill of the bus drivers and the thoughtfulness of the tourists. If a driver approaches a cheetah at an angle—kind of sneaking up on it—and does not try to get too close, the cheetah may not abandon its kill. If the tourists are quiet, they probably will not disturb the cheetah.

Tourists may present a unique and difficult problem to cheetah mothers. Tourists especially love to see baby cheetahs. At least one scientist believes that predators such as hyenas may learn that where there are tourists, there are likely to be cheetah cubs. The hyenas can follow the tourist vehicles, find the cubs, and eat them.

Because cheetahs face so many dangers in the wild, zoos and animal parks are trying to breed them in captivity. But raising these beautiful cats, zookeepers have discovered, is not an easy task.

Tourists watch as a cheetah and her cubs hunt in Kenya's Masai Mara Game Reserve. In the wild or in zoos, cheetahs fascinate people.

Chapter 7

A Zookeeper's Headache

Cheetahs are among the most popular animals at zoos. They are beautiful. They are graceful. And everyone knows they are very, very fast. But modern zoos are more than places where people can see beautiful animals. They are our last hope of saving the world's most endangered species.

Up until about 1950, whenever zookeepers wanted to display animals, they simply hired someone to catch them in the wild. Many of these animals died of stress or other causes soon after their capture. The zoos would have more animals taken from the wild until some managed to survive. So, along with hunting and habitat destruction, zoos once contributed to the loss of wild animals.

Many wild animals are endangered, just as the cheetah is. Modern zoos are committed to protecting these animals. Zookeepers try to learn all they can about the animals for which they are responsible. They must know how to take care of the animals and keep them healthy. They must provide natural-looking enclosures to make the animals comfortable. And they must try to breed the animals, so that animals for study and exhibit are born in captivity, rather than taken from the wild. Some zoos are even releasing animals back into the wild. The Arabian oryx, the golden lion tamarin, and the California condor are three animals that have been successfully released into their natural habitats by zoos.

Planning for Survival

Animals in zoos cannot leave their enclosures to find mates. They depend on zookeepers to arrange that. Managing the mating of so many animals can get confusing. So the American Association of Zoological Parks and Aquariums (AAZPA) set up the Species Survival Plans (SSP) program to supervise the breeding of zoo animals. SSPs have been set up for endangered animals, as well as for animals that are not endangered but that are rare in captivity.

There is an SSP for each species, including one for cheetahs. The SSP committee decides what is best for the health and preservation of the particular species under its care. Each zoo in the AAZPA must agree to abide by the SSP committee's decisions. The committee members consult with experts on nutrition, behavior, reproduction, infectious diseases, and genetics to make sure the animals stay in the best of health.

The cheetah SSP committee keeps detailed breeding records on the approximately 300 cheetahs for which it is responsible. It uses these records to decide which cheetahs should be mated. The committee avoids having the same pair mate several times because they do not want captive cheetahs to become more inbred than they already are. If many cubs all have the same parents, the species' genetic diversity will decrease even further.

Each SSP committee treats the animals in all the zoos in North America as if they were one large population. Often a committee decides that two animals from different zoos should be mated. Then one of the animals must be moved to the zoo where the other one lives. If the cheetah SSP committee decides that a cheetah should move from the San Diego Zoo to the Cincinnati Zoo, the cheetah goes, regardless of which zoo owns the animal.

A cheetah walks the boundary of its enclosure in New Orleans'
Audubon Zoo.

Caring for Captive Cheetahs

Cheetahs are not easy to care for. Male cheetahs, unless they are brothers, tend to be loners. Unrelated males fight when kept together in the same enclosure. At De Wildt Cheetah Breeding and Research Facility in South Africa, keepers solved this problem by putting several litters of very young male cheetahs together. They found that when unrelated male cheetahs grow up together, they live peacefully with one another as adults. Adult females, however, must always be kept separately, each in her own enclosure, and out of sight of male cheetahs.

Zookeepers must be very careful with the cheetahs' diet. If their food contains too few vitamins and minerals, the cats' health suffers. If their food lacks copper, cubs' backs become rounded. If they don't have enough of the vitamin thiamine, the cubs stagger and have convulsions.

Sometimes there are too many hormones in the cheetahs' food. Hormones are substances produced by living cells that control a variety of functions in plants and animals. In the early 1980s, captive cheetahs in zoos throughout the United States were having liver problems, and some of the females became infertile. Zookeepers were puzzled. Cheetahs in captivity in South Africa did not have these problems. When researchers compared the diets of the two captive populations, they discovered that cheetahs in the United States were fed horsemeat, but the South African animals were not. The horsemeat was found to contain high levels of estrogen, a hormone that affects reproduction. The horses got the estrogen from the plants they ate. Zookeepers in the United States took the cheetahs off their diet of horsemeat. Instead, they began feeding the cats chicken, which did not contain estrogen. The cheetahs' health improved.

Zookeepers also worry about the cheetah's low resistance to

disease. In captivity, cheetahs live much closer to one another than they would in the wild. To prevent sick cats from infecting one another, cheetahs must be kept away from other zoo cats that might pass on a disease.

More than 40 zoos in North America keep cheetahs. If a group at one zoo does get sick, not all the cheetahs in captivity will get sick. But zookeepers sometimes send cheetahs from zoo to zoo, for exhibit or for breeding. When they do, they are very careful. They try to make sure that no sick animals go from one zoo to another.

One Cheetah + One Cheetah = More Cheetahs?

From the earliest times, cheetahs in captivity have been difficult or impossible to breed. Although Akbar the Great kept many cheetahs in captivity, only one of them was reported to have had cubs.

Even in modern times, cheetahs have been extremely difficult to keep in captivity. In the first half of the twentieth century, 30 percent of the adults captured in the wild and brought to zoos died within six months. Cheetahs were also poor breeders. It was not until 1956 that keepers at the Philadelphia Zoo were able to get a cheetah to produce offspring in captivity. Since then, only 10 to 15 percent of the female cheetahs caught in the wild have had cubs in captivity.

Zookeepers have begun to understand some of the cheetah's problems with breeding. Researchers have found that cheetahs are more likely to breed if they live in natural surroundings. They like having high places on which to sit and look everything over, just as cheetahs do on the plains. They need room to get away from each other if they want to, and room to run.

Although cheetahs cannot hunt other animals in zoos, they seem to like being able to watch antelopes grazing in nearby enclosures.

Researchers have noticed that female cheetahs are choosy about their mates. Keepers cannot simply put a female and a male together and expect them to produce cubs. The female cheetah has to be able to pick a mate from among several males, or she may not mate at all.

Zookeepers also must be sure that all the males a female meets are fertile. Before they started testing males for fertility, zookeepers made some mistakes. Some selected the females' potential mates by looking for the strongest and handsomest male cheetahs. But these good-looking cats were often infertile. When researchers began testing males for fertility, they found that often the scruffiest-looking males turned out to be the best breeders.

When a female is ready to mate, zookeepers arrange to let her see the males. At the Oklahoma City Zoo, that means the female cheetahs get a ride in the Cheetah Wagon. The wagon is 8 feet long, 3 feet wide, and 4 feet high, and looks something like a horse trailer. The keepers put food in the wagon to persuade the female to get into it. Then they hook the trailer to a scooter, and off they go to the males' enclosure! The advantage of the Cheetah Wagon is that keepers do not have to tranquilize the female to move her. Tranquilizing an animal can be very stressful, or even fatal. But the cheetahs also seem to enjoy the ride, according to their keeper.

Sometimes zoos trade or borrow animals when it's time to breed their cheetahs. There are two reasons for this. The keepers must avoid having the same pair mate each time. Also, a zoo that has only infertile male cheetahs has to borrow fertile males—or send its females to other zoos—if the females are to have cubs.

Some scientists think that abnormal sperm cause infertility in male cheetahs. Other scientists think the problem is more complicated. Some male cheetahs seem to be able to father cubs in the wild, but not in captivity. And sometimes the fertility of captive cheetahs changes. One zoo sent a male cheetah to another zoo for breeding. He was fertile when he left the first zoo but not when he got to the second zoo. The opposite can happen, too. Sometimes just a change of location can cause an infertile male to become fertile. No one understands why.

Despite the problems, zookeepers have become more successful in rearing and breeding cheetahs in captivity. There are more than 300 cheetahs at zoos and wild animal parks in North America. More than 20 facilities are trying to breed the cats. Yet zoos cannot encourage too much breeding. In the United States, there is only enough room at zoos and wild animal parks to house about 320 cheetahs. Zookeepers are careful to control the size of the captive cheetah population while making sure there will be enough cheetahs for zoo visitors to enjoy and learn from in the future.

Two cheetahs hunt in tall grass.

Epilogue

The sun is setting on the Serengeti Plains. In the shade of a thorn-covered bush lie a mother cheetah and her two five-month-old cubs. The female hunted successfully today. The stomachs of the three cats are full and round. The mother purrs loudly as she licks one cub's face. The other stands, puts his forepaws on his mother's shoulders, and gazes at the Tommies munching grass in the distance.

In a tourist lodge nearby, excited visitors talk about their day over dinner. Today they saw what they came all the way to Africa hoping to see. Through their binoculars they watched a cheetah stalk its prey. In a sudden burst of speed, so quick they could hardly follow it, the cheetah dashed through the sun-burned grass and killed an antelope. These modern visitors were as thrilled by the sight as were crowds in India more than a thousand years ago.

In a tent camp on the plains, a scientist writes up his notes as the sun sets. He, too, watched the cheetah make her kill this afternoon. He is studying the cheetahs, hoping to understand them and add a little more to human knowledge about these amazing cats.

Despite pressure from all sides, cheetahs continue to be crowd pleasers. They fascinate scientists, zookeepers, and the public alike. They present endless puzzles to researchers who study cheetah genetics, evolution, and reproduction. Keepers are charmed by what biologist George Schaller called "this gentle, elegant cat." The public longs to see the cheetah's incredible, blazing speed. They fall in love with the cat's grace and dignity.

Although cheetahs are threatened by predators, humans, disease, lack of genetic diversity, and poor fertility, there is hope that they will survive. As understanding and appreciation of cheetahs grow, people will want to ensure that the world's fastest animal does not run into extinction.

Glossary

allele—one variety of a particular gene. In humans, one gene determines blood type, but there are three different blood-type alleles: A, B, and O.

chromosomes—long chains of genes

coalition—a small group of male cheetahs that help each other get food or defend a territory

DNA (deoxyribonucleic acid)—the molecule that carries the genetic code that gives living things their special characteristics

estrus—the time in a female cheetah's reproductive cycle during which she can become pregnant

genes—the basic units of heredity. Each gene provides coded instructions for one or more hereditary traits, such as disease resistance. A particular trait may be determined by one or by many genes.

home range—a large, undefended geographical area. Female cheetahs and non-territorial male cheetahs live in home ranges.

immunoglobulins—proteins that destroy invaders, such as viruses or bacteria, in the blood. Immunoglobulins are also called antibodies.

inbreeding—the mating of closely related individuals

mantle—the mane that extends from the nape of a young cheetah's neck to the base of its tail

nomads—single or immature male cheetahs that travel over huge home ranges rather than defending a territory

Pleistocene epoch—a period in the earth's history from about 1.7 million to 10,000 years ago

population bottleneck—an event that reduces the number of animals in a species so far that the species nearly becomes extinct

social—living in groups

solitary—living alone

territory—a small geographical area defended by an animal against others of its own kind. Territorial male cheetahs mark the edges of their territories by spraying urine on shrubs, trees, and grass.

Selected Bibliography

Caro, T. M. *Cheetahs of the Serengeti Plains.* Chicago: University of Chicago Press, 1994.

Eaton, Randall. *Cheetahs: The Biology, Ecology, and Behavior of an Endangered Species.* New York: Van Nostrand Reinhold, 1974.

Frame, George W. and Lory Herbison Frame. *Swift and Enduring: Cheetahs and Wild Dogs of the Serengeti.* New York: E. P. Dutton, 1981.

_____. "Our Three Years with the Cheetahs." *International Wildlife,* January/February 1977, 4-10.

_____. "Cheetahs: In a Race for Survival." *National Geographic,* May 1980, 712.

Kitchener, Andrew. *The Natural History of the Wild Cats.* Ithaca, NY: Cornell University Press, 1991.

O'Brien, Stephen, David E. Wildt, and Mitch Bush. "The Cheetah in Genetic Peril." *Scientific American,* May 1986, 84-92.

Schaller, George B. "This Gentle and Elegant Cat." *Natural History,* June/July 1970, 30.

Seidensticker, John, and Susan Lumpkin, eds. *Great Cats: Majestic Creatures of the Wild.* Emmaus, PA: Rodale Press, 1991.

Wrogeman, Nan. *Cheetah Under the Sun.* New York: McGraw-Hill, 1975.

Metric Conversion Factors

When you know	multiply by	to find
inches	2.5	centimeters
feet	0.30	meters
yards	0.91	meters
miles	1.6	kilometers
pounds	0.45	kilograms
°Fahrenheit	0.56 (*after* subtracting 32)	°Celsius

Index

*Pages listed in **bold** type refer to photographs.*

Photo Acknowledgments

Photographs reproduced with the permission of: Tom Brakefield, pp. 1, 6, 10, 22, 26, 29, 35, 36, 38, 40, 57, 60, 67, 82; Michele Burgess, pp. 2–3, 9, 30, 46, 48, 53, 54, 59, 74; Gerard Lemmo, p. 15; Scala/Art Resource, NY, p. 19; Wildlife Safari/Johnson, p. 21; Karlene V. Schwartz, p. 77; Noella Ballenger, p. 88. Map on page 13 and cheetah fur graphic by Laura Westlund.

Cover photographs reproduced with the permission of: Tom Brakefield, front; Brian Vikander, back.

Sharon Elaine Thompson with Boytjie, at De Wildt Cheetah Breeding and Research Center, South Africa

About the Author

Sharon Elaine Thompson has been fascinated by cheetahs since she first saw one run on a television documentary. It was a dream come true when she met a full-grown, hand-raised cheetah at De Wildt Cheetah Research and Breeding Facility in South Africa, and scratched him under his chin. He purred.

Thompson has written more than 100 articles about jewelry and gemstones; copper mining; singing sand dunes; gorillas, chimps, rhinos, and cheetahs; and all kinds of people. In her quest for stories, she has visited the Namib Desert of Africa and the gem mining areas of Brazil. She has written three other books, including *Death Trap: The Story of the La Brea Tar Pits*.

Thompson has lived all over the United States and in Kyoto, Japan. She now lives in Oregon. When she is not writing, she reads, paints, walks, quilts, and tries to control the dandelions in her yard.